LOS ANGELES 90049   FEB. 16/2019

Dear "Pres. Ed" — WESTERN MICHIGAN
                                      UNIVERSITY
Enjoy Poems-of-life/ Faces-of-Poems"
"good Reading" — ADVOCACY — etc.

Such a pleasure meeting you, + visiting
for a while &

good Health,
god willing —

(James) Byron Clark

"POEMS THE FACES"
"WORDS OF POEMS"

"Thouahts & Ideas"

"Forms"

"Fold & Flow & Freedom"

"Essay"

"Anecdotes"

"Suppositions"

Poems of "Prophecies" & References

"Tasteful. Flavor & Favor"

"Policy/Political"

"Advocacy"

Poems a.k.a "Soap Box"

"Whimsical"

Nostalaia & whatever/so forth

Ergo/a.k.a/ie/hubris/circa/veracity

p.s (1) One "naughty" poem

(2) Another one "naughty" poem

by

~Byron Clark~

"Eva" Good Witch

"POEMS OF LIFE / POEMS THE FACES"

Avid Readers Publishing Group
http://www.avidsreaderspg.com
ISBN Numbers #

jbc
rev. oct, 18, 2018
los angeles, 90049

HOLLYWOOD
Book Reviews

Title: ***Poems of Life / Faces of Poems***
Author: **Byron Clark**
Publisher: Avid Readers Publishing Group ISBN-13:978-1-61286-260-6
Genre: Autobio Poetry
Pages: 100
Reviewed by: ***Jodi Gallagher*** / **Book Critic/ News Review**

Hollywood Book Reviews

I was fortunate to receive my copy of "*Poems of Life/ Faces of Poems*" in its hardcover version signed by the author *(Jim) Byron Clark*. A nice welcoming to my journey paging the poetry/ quotations, musings, aphorisms, autobio reflections and captioned photographs.

Poems of life/ Faces of Poems reads like a "stream of consciousness"- - jumping from personal memoires of people from *Byron Clark's* life, his travels, parties and family and friends. Always handsome and dapper in of photographs, *Mr. Clark* appears the life of royalty. Whether he's wearing a denim shirt, bandana and cowboy hat outside a stable in Santa Barbara or white dinner jacket or tuxedo in Rome. He's always dressed appropriately for the occasion!

Book Reviews

(1)

He is toasting with a cocktail or glass of champagne in his hand, along with the "who's who" of _celebrity personalities_ of the time period. The book has the genre of a scrapbook style, clips of photos and comments placed around the gallery text of the pages. Even the typestyle and font coloration is _whimsical_ in nature, adding a layer of creativity and fun to the book. I (particularly) liked the poem about his poodle, _"Peaches Apricot Poodle a.k.a. Black-Eyes Princess"_ in that poem, the spelling of _"dog"_ as being backwards for **_"God,"_** and shows the _love_ and _devotion_ for each other. _Byron's_ love and respect for his wife is "showcased" in everything he does when rejoices with his wife _Eleanor Vallee!_ Friends from all professions and acquaintances around the world/ it are easy to drift into the optimism and humble kindness of _Byron Clark's_ world!

A cornucopia of revelations, **Poems _of Life/ Faces of Poems_** is a book which is a must have possession to all those touched by _Byron Clark_ throughout his _bon vivant life_! To others it is an ideal way to get to know the author and be swept into the _"Noman Rockwell" America_ which he lived throughout! He was an "official ambassador" to the countries visited, a scholarly _influence_ to his _friends_, and most of all an _honest_ person with good _principles_. Having a signed copy of his work of art will now become a valued keepsake in my personal library. _Clark's remarkable ability_ to express himself in a _raw_ and _honest manner_ lets you not only read his experiences, but also join in! _Every poem_ was an absolute _delight_ that _appealed_ to me in _wit_, _heartbreak_ and _adventure_!

I highly recommend looking for a _"good read"_; you will find not only _poetry_, but also a _feeling_ of _camaraderie_ with the _author_ himself.....

Jodi Gallagher/Reviewer
Book Critic/ News Review
Hollywood Book Reviews
July 16, 2018

Book Reviews

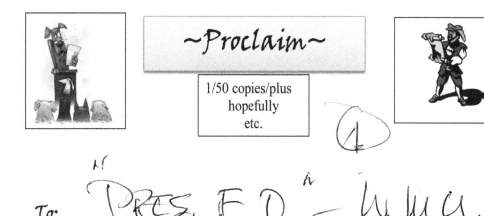

~Proclaim~

1/50 copies/plus
hopefully
etc.

To: _____ PRES. ED — M.M.C.

Buyer

Enjoy *"Poems of Life"* / *"Faces of Poems"* &
"Good reading"... thoughtfully ... obdurate
and tacit-observation...

Good Health,
God Will...

Signed: (Jim) Byron Clark

jbc
los angeles, 90049

~ POEMS OF LIFE ~

of "Thoughts & Ideas"
of "Forms"
of "Fold & Flow & Freedom"
of "Essay"
of "Anecdotes"
of "Suppositions
Poems of "Prophecies" & References
of "Tasteful, Flavor & Favor"
of "Policy/Political"
of "Avocacy"
Poems a.k.a "Soap Box"
of "Whimisical"
"Nostalgia & Words" & Others
Ergo/a.k.a/ie/hubris/circa/veracity

p.s (1) One "naughty" poem
(2) Another One "naughty" poem

A "Scribe"

"Eva" Good Witch

by

Byron Clark

<u>Dedication</u>

Lena B Clark, Monticellonian. . .
Love and Beloved and certainly
appreciated in Monticello Drew County Arkansas.

She was a devout Christian. . . active in Monticello
First Southern Baptist Church / my mother was there!
". . .the meek shall inherit the earth
the deeds that men do live after them. . ."

Lena was always supporting me. . . my choice,
career, encouragement, & *acting* my avocation of life.
Lena was a <u>*Godly*</u> woman, *dedicated*, and *integrity*.
She was/is/ my *Star*. . . my *Mother*.

Homer J. Clark, my *Pop*, charming, handsome,
intelligent, honest, and guts. *I Love Him*. . .
People liked *Him*. . . He liked *Them*!
Lena adored *Homer* and both lovingly-loved. . .
God *blessed all of us*!
". . .but deliver us from evil
for thine is the kingdom,
and the power and the glory
forever and ever. . . Amen" *

Eleanor Vallee Clark. . .
And she came into <u>my life</u>. . .
Beautiful, tall, aristocratic her head so proud
The impish. darling smile
Her giving, wonderful laugh. . .
So special, so dear - - love, cherish & "one"
Caring for all. . . Aquarian . . .
That's "<u>Ellie</u>. . ." My <u>Dear</u> / My <u>Wife</u>. . . I Love <u>You</u>!

~ james byron clark ~
los angeles 90049
july 10, 2014

* Lord's *Prayer*

About the Author:

PROFILE:

BYRON CLARK

Author Fade In:Time-Line/Earlier Years 1950's

Byron Clark, B.S. Degree and Theatre,Western Michigan University, Kalamazoo, Mich. As active actor during productions of WMU, Ms. Shaw. And the Summer-Stock, "The Barn Theatre," Augusta, Mich. with Michael (Capanna) Keep, Margaret Curran,Milt Hammerman, Alicia Krug, Bill Flatley, Lou Cutell . . . wonderful talent. Also, productions in Kalamazoo Civic Theatre, Madge Skelly & Karl Genus, Dirs.; and *Byron* performing in "Remains to Seen," the "Imaginary Invalid," by Moliere among others . . . Soon a position as Editor/ Writer with Douglas Aircraft Co. in Los Angeles, California. Full time job, intrigue, artistic, prosaic, and tiring, continue assistance, acting "Little Theatre," "Off-Broadway." As soon "on-to-New York" striving, studying, and working as actor in New York City (5years) . . . Back to Los Angeles.

(Fade-In: Time -Line/Later Middle Years 1970's-2014

Editor/Collaborating/Writer with Byron Clark (as) literary-labor & monetary advancing for *a named Publisher* accomplishment. Collaborative, Editing/grammar, typo's, writing etc . . . *"styling -completes"* for presenting, writing, knowledge, reading additional supplement for *"polish"* this book: *"Cyrus the Great"* Ahasuerus . . . Ergo, important interesting this heavy *Venue* includes intrigue, intrinsic, artistic, and especially *nuance* rich *mythology* of Ancient Roman Civilization with irrefragable Prophecies . . ."**Gravatis**" Commercial honing-presentation… ***"Cyrus the Great" Ahasuerus***.
Reference Bible Stories: . . . *"Babylon"*. . . *"Tower of Babel"* . . . *"Ancient*)

Byron an actor with a varied background including Summer Stock, Off Broadway, Television commercials and films. Credits include "The Fall Guy, "The Judge," "Superior Court," "Capital," "Divorce Court," and re-occurring roles in "Knots Landing," and "Dallas." His film roles include "The Man Killers," "The Stepdaughters," "The Abominable Snowman," "Weekend of Terrors" and "Protocol." Mr. Clark is active in voice/overs and movie trailers. Currently he tours with Eleanor Vallee (Rudy Vallee's widow) in the stage presentation of "Love Letters" and also on cruise lines. Byron is originally from Monticello, Arkansas. *Mr. Clark* lives with his wife, Eleanor and their apricot poodle, Princess Peaches & Baby Princess white maltese in the Brentwood area of Los Angeles 90049. . . Alan Watts and e.e. cummings' works are influential in my writings. Mr. Watts *is* and *was* an "icon" with *"Western-Eastern" Zen* works, including *The Wisdom of Insecurity* among other books . . . Byron Clark, four (4) poems of series, "Our Life," "Awakening," "Shane," "The Vigil, Ode to Ben Tucker," & published the International Who's Who in Poetry.Com, Howard Ely, Editor. . . 1 Plaza Owings Mills, Maryland, 21117.

James Byron Clark
~ Los Angeles ~
April 28th, 2014

"Eva" Fairchild

Fade-In: Time-Line /Presently Years 2008-2014

Artistic Graphic Editor. . . Visual *"styling*-completes"
pictures, pictorials and *breath-like* into <u>vital</u>, <u>vitalize,</u>
<u>vibrant</u>, *into efforts*. Multi-organization to bring-about
"Poems of <u>life</u>," *book-life:* Time-Line to (for) *History.* . .
Eva Fairchild, fondly & good-friend, and accomplishment
efforts & adroitly 'bringing-my-book,' "<u>Poems-of-Life</u>" to
alive. . .

Also, multi-choice-talented & other expertise and life-long
resident of Malibu. . . *"Eva"* provides exceptional depth of
knowledge and *professionalism* of the area. Apropos, to her
Los Angeles clients, the team of *The Partner Trust Group*
and the also *International Clients*, etc. Todos Santos,
Mexico, & Cabo surrounding areas and venue . . . plus!

Michael Reyes:

Designer/Director/ Computer Creative Tech/
Consultant Art Graphic Designs inclusive:
multi-choices, as per tacit talent. . .
Kudos, dittos for ***Mike Reyes***, amazing Computer Creative Tech Graphics of **"*Poems of Life.*"** This
is appreciatively & helpfully & such dogmatic & abundant efforts. . . such as: *Artistic & Artesian.* . .

Mary Ann Vitto & "Baby-Bailey", Maltese

<u>Fade-In: Semi-edit rev. / oct 18, 2018</u>

Top-caliber Computer Creative *Graphic Editor*. Artistic adroitly
extra-help for Design "<u>Poems-of-Life</u> / Faces of Poems" for
venue-milieu style. <u>Kudos</u> again, "<u>dittos</u>" for **Mary Ann Vitto**/
such dogmatic & grand efforts & such artistic and artesian.
.... <u>Personal/Asst.</u> & *"Baby-Bailey"* doggy-<u>sitter</u>/ <u>Royalty!</u>

jbc
<u>rev.</u> oct 18, 2018
los angeles, 90049

"Poems of Life" / "Poems of Faces"

"Baby-Bailey" say's,

"Please follow the paws

to the following pages. . ."

*Bessie Bailey/namesake
jbc/mr

*   "Baby-Bailey"

About the Book

"Poems of Life"/"Words of Poems"

(1) | Plethora |

Some "*Faces of Poems*" . . . some "*Poems of Life*"
Thoughts of Ideas/ Tasteful Flavor & Favor/circa: *Hannibal/
Roma/ "Quintus Fabius Maximus"*/admin. "*community organizer*"
"**acorn**" spoiler 'Fabian'/ anti-military & appeasement-incompetent/
supposition: "wants" delusions-disconnected our *u.S.A*
"leading-from-the-back,"/ behind! . . . *pre-disposed*:assimilation
subliminal/ (6)earlier years/Indonesian religion/culture/supposition/
"emperor" "*closet-muslim*" venues/ *hubris...* "*no one will find out*". . .

Poem Narrative Essay/ "*Fantasy Supposition*"
~ Remembering/Remembrance/Recollection ~

| Cacophony | (2)

"Early Morning/Twilight Feelings/Sub-Conscious/Conscious"
*Sotto Word Sounds: Rewired/Semi-Wired/Yang-Wang/
Switch-Witch/ Cling-Clang/Wick-Quake/Frick-Frack*. . .
Fold & flows & freedom/assign compile aligned/completion. . .
In *words-of-progress*/ ergo: erudition, acumen, idyllic, exigent,
herculean, ethos; excelsior, literal, litany, literate, eureka, essayist,
gargantuan, c/o poems/ supposition/ but tacit. . . ref: loquacious!

(3) | Potpourri |

Gravitas/Honing/Poems "*Good Reading*," Informative,
Whimsical, "Ideal-Thoughts…" Policy/ Politics & now &
Prophecies & Reference; "Soap-Box" & whatever/so forth!
Advocacies/cosmic-brain mimic puppetry/ public pandering venue . . .
P.S. (1) One "Naughty" Poem ~ (2) Two "Naughty" Poem ~

Thanks & *Enjoy* (my)"*Poems of Life*" aka "*Poems of Pictures*" etc. . .

(1) *excessive amount*
(2) *unpleasant noise*
(3) *mixture things*

jbc

The Generals

Gail   "Ellie"   Poppy

Lubie   Timmie   Kathy

"The Impossibles"

TABLE OF CONTENTS

Saga 1 / "Poems of Life" / "Poems of Faces"

THE END

"Poems of Life"/ "Poems of Faces"

"Poems of Drawings" /"Poems of Films"

"Words of Poems"

L-R   Billy Carson, Dansby White, Byron Clark, Billy Marks, Wayne Jordan, James Veasey

"Boys-of-Summer"/ memories-nostalgic "Faces of Poems"

"Our Life"

Life just plunges on
Minute by minute
Hour by hour, day by day.

Like a beautiful, wild white Stallion.
"Today is yesterday
Yesterday is today"
And another day is <u>saturday</u>
And <u>tomorrow</u> is always there!

We are like *hostages* on a huge,
beautiful, white, glittering
Ferris wheel.
All in-and-out-of-control
"<u>Waiting</u> . . . For the Giant-ticket-man"
To *Punch* us-out-on his *<u>Patrol!</u>*

james byron clark
2005 los angeles 90049

youtube: Byron Clark

Juxtaposes

Young/ & younger years ago

a-far a-faraway just around

a-walking toward right to

"a slight vine covered -steps-up-to- hill"

library around the corner

"misty dream" "ideal Love"/

"lovely ideal"

cognitive change

potpourri

supposition "Fantasy"/but...

walking in/on/old campus across

Vandercook/WMU/Kalamazoo...

Erotic, steaming, secret, silent/

raw sexual & sensual & emotions/

"body-heat" romantic carnal milieu

" a walk to remember"

.....a waiting long!/wanting...

toknowhowtoolong? fringements/

fragment/ stutter/pernicious/obdurate

stoic and..."Ideal Love"/ Ideal-ly Love

.....becomes... / Ideal-ly-Less...

'Closure'... just Less... Fini/ 'the End'...

"tu es trop"...? MD

juxtaposes

NEWS/FLASH/"La Dolce Vita" femminile/Anita Ekberg passato over/ Jan/11/2015

Rocca di Papa, Italy / Trevi Fountain/ Rome .... -CAPUT-

P.S. Marcello Mastroianni....

ONWARD FORWARD/OXYMORON...*

*figure of speech that juxtaposes elements misnomer that
appear to be the contradictory/ locution produces an incongruous,
seemingly self-contradictory effect... redundant!

jbc
rev.july 18, 2018
los angeles,90049

~ *Awakening Love* ~

Singapore

Awakening...
Semi-darkness, light seeping through
the heavy brocade, Versailles drapes -
Awakening with bewilderment, anxiety,
gut-feelings pushing through...
What to do?
To push out...Where?
New breath...New life?
Or stay, in prison...
Subdued...

And she came into my life -
Beautiful, tall, aristocratic her head so proud
The impish, darling smile -
Her giving, wonderful laugh...

So special, so dear -- love, cherish & "one"
Caring for all...Aquarian...
That's "Ellie..."
My Dear - **My Wife**...I Love You!

poetry.COM

~ james byron clark ~
los angeles 90049
june 2006

pg. 2

"Peaches" Apricot Poodle
a.k.a
'Black-Eyes Princess'

'Black-eyed peas eyes' gal my apricot-red, beautiful, <u>poodle</u>,
trustful, wild-world class, royal loveable, and <u>loves me</u>!
so wildly calm playful and guide, and <u>somewhat guile</u> !
always gratis and loyal, always wired and *gives more!*
She's always there . . . and never late
"kisses and hugs" to us . . .

Looking at those 'black- eyed peas eyes'
Does she understand? Or not? She must know . . .
Seemingly so! I think we know . . . I think so . . .
I know so! **God** knows now . . . We know . . . now we do!

Those **God**-like eyes . . .'black-eyed peas' that's my 'our'
Apricot Peaches Princess Vallee-Clark with dark-eyes poodle,
'our daughter'. . . our darling and sweet
girl and delicate, delectable
through thought dark eyes talking our deity <u>Peaches</u>
<u>God</u> . . . **<u>Dog</u>** backward/ "**<u>GOD</u>**" spell/we did so . . . We know now So?

We <u>love</u> you always . . . you think so ? You do so !
Merri merry smiling eyes adorable beautiful face
'Fu- man- chu' demeanor eyes face always close to us. . .
But ? . . . yes . . . maybe ? . . . yes!
One day <u>Doggie</u>-Spiritually- **God** . . . not <u>c</u>losed /<u>always open</u> . . .

james byron clark

P.S. "<u>Baby Bailey</u>" Princess
<u>Poem to be soon . . . .</u>

~ *"Villa Eleanor" Cocktail- Time* ~   ~ June 10th, 2009   Los Angeles ~ ~90049

'Your Best Shot"
Potpourri

so what happen . . .
when you've given . . .
"your best shot!"
are you there? what you care? on top?
aware . . . beware!

element of dreams passes & madness
do you believe . . . how you feel?
can toward beautiful beauty come- about
such a price . . . you stand &
"strive & thrive at length your very weakness
becomes the pillar of your strength"

"life ain't no crystal staircase
such as splinters & torn-up more-worn-out
wooden & tacks . . . wearing out!
so . . . potpourri . . . ergo apropos

* "when you do reach
the mountain-tops
'wag-way' the courage
to the other 'ones' in the foothills . . ."

so you're there! do you care? really? Your best shot!
where ever you go there you are / you'll be there!
"oh! s'wonderful s'marvelous" ~george gershwin
"i can't get started" ~bix beiderbecke & bunny berigan

meaningful & spiritual & all
aw . . aw . . c'est la vie . . so/potpourri/maybe so!

zen feeling? what is zen?
'fist-punch in face . . . alan watts ref:
epiphany "the wisdom of insecurity" . . ."

"naw me re nay kwo ko"
(phonetically)
"namu myco renge kyo . . ."have a nice week"

james byron clark
december 6th, 2010
orient express far-east
~ Singapore ~

* me & anonymous

pg. 4

Granduer Pink Lady

Scene 5:30am: fade in face/quiet dark warm /fog clean
fresh breath /island/up high
tower pink balcony a soft smooth time-warm
breeze earlier-morn / with early morning
semi- darkness above / below over -cast
sweet- smells ocean-air mellifluous a misty-rain
mélange with moody warm feelings
spitting splitting the infinite straight horizon
skylight heavenly-line azure ocean . . .

Cut to pov (1):
below small moist-wet pearl-pink sandy beach
small figures below/ majestic huge
green grey whale-like "diamond-head"
listening . . . protective . . . superstitious . . .
looking the distance . . . holding /forth guardian . . .
God-like . . .

Cut to pov (2):
semi-dawn down-below beach boys figures
setting-up sofa-ish blue cabanas cacophony
challenging raising riding enjoying aqua waves
in the straight smooth strength protective-paladin/cherish
this 'zen' epiphany/ with tasty famous /infamous 'mai tais'
"Ellie & Byron" and other 'church goers . . .'

Cut to pov (3):
unboards out-board riggers long boats
preparing sun-thirsty 'main-liners' j-crew to lounge
bond/abound the now know 'ledgable' well-known
the sun will reknown knowledgeable 'the sun will shine'

Cut to pov (4)
slendering skinny towering plethora nau coconut palms
covering deep blue pool and pink cabanas ringing around
nostalgic remembrance legend rooster/ "kanhelemona" flew down
furiously challenging scratching earth at 'kakuhihema's' ruler feet/ land "helumoa"
staunch strong over hundred years long "pink lady" aka 'pink palace'
ergo "the queen" albeit "hawaiian renaissance" culture sovereign
iconic "The Royal Hawaiian . . ." and royal & loyal . . .

Mahalo & Aloha . . .
fini . . . a keeper/wrap !

The Royal Hawaiian

Legend rooster "kanhelemona"
down scratching earth
ruler feet "kakuhihema"/ land "helumoa"

  "Ellie"

James Byron Clark
November 11th, 2011 ~ Honolulu ~
Eleanor Vallee

"Shane"

And "**Shane**" came into my life
like a fresh, laughing spring smile.
Wobbling, tentative unsure steps . . .
With style . . . a Baby

Such a small bundle
Could give such happiness
So giving and wanting
Growing and evolving to
Such a beautiful girl, woman,
Elegant lady.

That's my long ago
And far-away Shane.

I <u>love</u> you
My daughter
<u>My</u> "**Shane**"

Drawing: "Shane"   *"Valentine Girl"*

~ Life is Probation ~

Our life is a probation
we are all "*probies*"
we are all coping striving
in the **God**-Spiritual-Heavenly Universe

Life is not meaning well but . . .
affirmation doing well
and "we strive and strive
and find at length
our very weakness has become
the pillar of our strength"

And now . . . some levity
Tongue-in-cheek (here)

"Screw the rest
be my guest Quest/
now take a rest . . .
be my Bequest" (profound) . . .

ref: Eva & james byron clark
Los Angeles / Feb 11th 2012

So . . .
remember what *peace* / *piece* that may be in *silence*
and as far as possible without surrender
be on good terms with all persons . . .
ergo i.e. & etc. apropos 'peoples' persons
speak always your "*truth*" quietly & clearly . . .

Special Tribute: "Lena"

Memorandum

"Lena Bailey Clark"
Aug. 7, 1907 - Apr. 23, 1975

Lena B. Clark **, Monticellonian** . . .
She was well known . . . Loved and Beloved
and <u>certainly</u> appreciated in Monticello
Drew County Arkansas . . . &
"other parts including Little Rock . . ."

Lena *was a devout Christian . . .*
active in the *Monticello First Baptist Church* . . .
Teaching 10-12 years year old girls Sunday School at one time.
In the early days from 'Pastor Crockston' to
'Pastor Washington' on into the 1970's . . .
Lena was there!
"*The meek shall inherit the earth*"
"*The deeds that men do live after them*"
Such was the case with my Mother . . .

Lena B. Clark (Sanderlin)
She worked <u>tirelessly</u> with <u>extended effort</u>
to help . . . <u>produce</u> and <u>procure</u> Jobs in
Monticello Drew County for the unemployed via the
<u>Ark. Employment Security Divisions</u> for over 30 years!

This included all groups:
White . . . Black . . . Latinos . . . Mexican and any other
"so-called diversified groups" one can think of . . . and so forth
This was way before the "goofy-propagandized 'P.C' . . ."
"<u>Politically</u> <u>Correct</u>" jazz/ <u>leftist</u> b.s.baloney fashionable . . .

Lena *was there!*
<u>Helping</u> . . . <u>Getting</u> <u>people jobs</u> . . .
"<u>Hometown Monticello.</u>"
That is, albeit, ***Lynvia Nichols*** *. . .* ***Virginia Brookings*** *. . .*
two other <u>sweet</u> and <u>most</u> <u>wonderful</u> ladies
and <u>thee</u> . . . ***Lena*** *. . . all <u>three</u> at the <u>Employment Office</u> did make*
a marked <u>contribution</u> to many ***<u>Monticellonians</u>*** *<u>lifes</u> . . . Encouragement & <u>Jobs</u>!*

Lena *was so pretty & beautiful . . . & so dear . . .*
She was ***<u>My Star</u>***!
<u>My Mother</u> !

~James Byron Clark~
August 2nd, 2010

pg. 8

~ The Dog Stays ~

"Coping"-- if it's not 'one' thing--
 it's another--
just as you get one "shoe" on . . .
the other one drops!

"Pop goes the weasel . . . "
and your wife leaves on/gone miserable
only along/ gong-gone-dong!
Where ever you go/there you are/ding-dong
The dog stays. . .

Ethos . . .
Cope & contain & compromise & coping/scoping
Conviviality & contingency
So who goes next?

"The pop goes weasel!"
You job is gone -- dong
mother-in-law-- ding
brother-in-law --dang

Declivity but Ergo: "Debinaire"
thank God --along --ding-dong/dang-pong . . .
1st chapter is not a complete book --
the door closes -- another opens &
2nd chapter on your narrative . . . the dogs stays!

"i don't want to set the world on fire"~ the ink spots
"send in the clowns" ~ lee ballard

"A womans' as allegory street car
life is just like another
one comes along every hour . . .
but it's always faster / taster
after midnight !"

Such as life/what ever/or ?
"a man tries at times distills certain
realities into wisdom". . .refine such as . . .
 such as life . . . not c'est la guerre
you're at home ! c'est la vie. . .

*The dog stays !

"Rufus"

"Street car named desire"

~ James Byron Clark ~
rev. july 18, 2018
Los Angeles, Calif. 90049

pg. 9

~Travelling ~

We are all travelling on that-line
fine-line stressing find-line love-line
hopefully-loving & faith strain-line
stain-line straight-light what do we do ? think~~
faith repeat "Rush dittos..." how can we ?
zen-alike flex-mode just go !

Ho! ho! ho! off to work we go! I don't know...
do you? so? Angels are flying above
"tick-tack-toe... white witches are alive!"

Life is precious... so cling God-spirit-within
inclusive "**passing-over**" is inclusive & conclusive
heaven -divine dying is "**exclusive**"
"amateurs" no professionals ... **travelling**
1st shot... 1st try... 1st attempt... **requited**!

By the way... "verily as I do! not as I say!"
not as I do ... you!
listen to voice ... your inner -internal clock
so? you know the way to go... trans/sistor

Ding! dong! the dark witch is dead... gone-gong!
along bing-bling-bong..."you're gone!" so be it !
"time after time" ~ Chet Baker ~
"time waits for no one/ it just passes you by"
tick! tack! toe! hickory dickory dock... time is gone !

'Its' **time** for the big " **Big Clock** ..." the "big-clang"
gong- bing -bong! bling -bong -gong ... "**you're gone!**"
Oh! my goodness! "ashes to cry" & go for the "**Heaven**"!
BEHOLD... NOW IS THE *SALVATION

"Eva" the "white witch"

* "666" End of Days...
God hopefully knows

james byron clark
june 10th, 2008
~ los Angeles 90049 ~

pg. 10

The Vigil, Ode to Ben Tucker

July 10th , 1925

October 13th , 2002

Ben Tucker, actor, mid 1960's

The **Mighty Warrior** is down on his knees
undaunted, unable to rise.
Inside, the Angel-like mother
and two Angel daughters fighting,
imploring, soothing,
grasping to keep the **Mighty Warrior** here, near.

The beautiful White Angel of Life is outside
hovering, waiting . . .

The Warrior-poet fighting, painfully grasping,
breathlessly grasping . . .
giving no quarter .

The Angel waiting for the heart
and soul to open, to acquiesce,
to say yes . . .to let go.

To be employed, enclosed -above
to the **Heavenly** Council of
Mighty Warriors on High . . .

The White Angel of Life
and the Angel of Death compromised.

And now . . . *Ben Tucker*
One **Handsome Mighty Warrior** Rises . . .

Ben's Legacy Mitie & Plummy

"Plummy" Tucker   "Mitie" Tucker

God-father child

Ben's (Pricilla) Legacy "Plummy" & "Mitie"

Saga 2/ Now. . .

Letters & Communiques/ Compliments/
Affirmative & Negative/ <u>Rebuttal</u> & etc/
Intermittently / Faces. . .

"Faces of Poems"/ Family

'Best' to <u>Phil</u> & <u>Izabela Gibson</u> &
'beautiful' Chloe & Cindy daughters

From the Sons of

Bijou

March 19, 2010

Dear Byron,

I was really touched and totally surprised by the Poem you wrote in honor of my Mother. I was *touched* by its sentiment and warm evocation of Mother's essence and "surprised" to discover you're a poet; and an accomplished one.

And I know Mother would've been deeply touched if you had read this to her. So the *closest* I can come to this, is, as I told you, to read this at the unveiling of her Headstone on June 22nd, the anniversary of her passing.

I'm sorry you and Ellie won't be there, but I know your thoughts will be with us. I read Tommy the Poem and he joins me in sending our heartfelt thanks to you for composing such a beautiful Tribute to Bijou, who you know loved you and Ellie very much. My love also...

Bijou

A charming, wonderful, sweet, bright, funny
"will-of-the-wisp" lovely artistic-type of . . .
Grand Dame . . . a Beautiful Lady.

*C*alifornian Beverly Hills, Hollywood knowledgeable.
Social -society events reaching out daily
Extending out, extending to all.

Giving, loving Edipus/Oedipus-Rex Triangle Three...
Two wonderful Sons . . . Bruce, Tommy and Thee . . .
All the Love and closeness
Through-out the years . . . These-Three.

A soft lush sun-blush frontal view
from the green tented on-cove . . .
Zen like geese touching down a little *
beyond on a gleaming, glittering lake . . .
not intending to leave a ripple nor
the lake intending to receive such . . .

*A*s Life's evening sun is sinking low
the purity white casket with enclosed
red roses with Sweet **Bijou** . . . is lowered below . . .
into the sod . . . unto the bosom of **God**. I must go . . .

* *To meet the deeds that I have done . . .
Where there will be no setting sun.

Tommy	Bijou	Bruce
Curtis	Durden	Cohen Curtis

. . . I Am . . .

* Allan Watts/sympathy

** **"Just as I am "**
Broadman Baptist Hymnal - 188

james byron clark
july 15th, 2009
~ los angeles ~

"stuttered" "clown" "actor"

Kelly

"Nero"

Byron . . . the stutter . . . actor
who can't shut up
for god sake
has heard enough
puff-- such stuff -- puff
"clown" "actor" just shut up. . .
all about conservative-policy/then politics
opinionated doubts opinions
agenda i.e. "politically correct" persons
ergo leftist "a community-organizer radical
closet--muslin" decisive pseudo diversity division
'multi-culture' alas caucasian-anglo white/misnomer
juxtaposed/african light medium dark "colored"/people of
colors ergo skin flavor favor fave shades negroid 'ditto'
afro-descendants albeit per se nigeria kenya rhodesia/somalia
zimbabwe and-all-before circa:"pas de deux"/nonparallel
asian -oriental among pakis @ illegal alien
american-mexican descents etc etc that is masses
central america bizarre/chaos/bankruptcy/u.s.a catastrophe
banality "3rd world browning of america" 'balderization'
mongrels aka wanting to American citizens sad but true . . .
pro-sematic & anti-sematic & ethic/ no racism/ reality
of truth. . . and spin . . . above said "p.c" no stutter . . . no!

capitalism adhesive work effort positive u.s.a
romney and is/was "melting pot" spirit-dream "contribution"
evolution fervent v.s.limousine liberal partisan aka 1st cuz "communist socialism
welfare-tax venue-policy no-veracity hubris marx "re-distribution" revolution diversity:
ps/pc addendum **english bilingual makes cripple earlier grade** a 'devoir'
bs . . . therefore such dogmatic dominate paramount "**full english immersion**"
mission . . . **speak english** !

los angeles sunshine
land of nuts & fruits
literally & figurally "out-of-sync"
sexual secularly social commentary
deviant debility de-bauchery
sodom and gomorrah w/o integrity
not-unlike "nero claudius fiddle grasping
burning for VI days the crown rome circa:
II ball & cane . . . phallus . . ."
los angeles u.s.a "city of angels"
"city of angels" u.s.a . . . light
los angeles mexico now . . . semi- darkness

all about soap-box
talk-talk . . .blah-blah . . .blabber
bumble. . .bearable babble. . .bungling
aware wired aware rewired sometimes . . .
of course subconsciously ~ nexus ~ cable . . .capable but . . .
only blatantly near-to-news informed
"following clowns"/ "circus-heads" well dressed swells . . .
wells . . .speaking strongly
iconlasts of the ref: french new wave . . .
avant-film caring sleeping waving
awakening mary janes roaches acid heads
strongly wrongly vapid vacuous ingenius
uncapable sociopolitical as they marching time
walking-along . . .being- strong
just talking . . .marking
now fallow-shallow . . .clinging-bang
meaning cling-clang . . .sounds . . . riposte- repartee . . . bs

Tragedy

Byron

pg. 16

alas dribble. . . diatribe dialouge:
hopefully maybe so . . . no
monologue: listen to the bore
tin-voice inning perfunctory . . .boar
basically pseudo false erudition in head

pertinent who knows maybe paranoid
i don't know doubtful afraid so . . .
so this kinda of a polly-wag
cacophony mix-mash plethora
of unconsciously . . . goofy-lackadaisical
staging . . . "paladin & patriarch" up tag
pandemic words down sag . . .
i don't know puff - such stuff- de facto. . .

/ "well what it's all about alfie"
"in other words fly me to the moon"
"send in the clowns"
"just as i am"
"the old rugged cross"
* "the passion of the christ"

lord byrons' bridge arch st. marks'
district venice embracing & spreading
branching labyrinth of white gleaming lights
clickering and clinging red and blue
engrossing enclosing a huge gigantic white
carousal and merri merry-go-round with . . .

12 **black** huge stallions **war horses**
with frosting blowing steam breath
from nostrils and **war horses**
going "up and down around and down again"
our beautiful magnificent **silky red rhône**
war horse front leading the stark frontal attack . . .

* *joey*

still distance is pastoral quite quiet pastoral . . .
heat-wave simmeringly field in powerful
* **rhone war horse**

stand-rear powerful legs first front hooves pawning dusty field . . .
front-up standing-up huge-freeze-frame
caring stable sensitive romantic beautiful large almond eyes
re-standing re-caring spiritual daunting-haunting-love with walf eerie
listening **albert** whistling lonesome sound **for joey** . . . listen . . .

* **joey wants to come home** . . .

" all is quiet on the western front" . . . transfixed
"path of glory" . . . transformed
" war horse" . . . transmorphing
"the passion of the Christ " . . . transrising . . .

~joey came home ~

* all quiet on the western front . . . lew ayres louis wolheim erich maria remarque ~ lewis milestone
* the path of glory . . . kirk douglas adolphe menjou george macready joe turkel ~stanley kubrick
* war horse . . . joey jeremy irvine albert michael morpurgo ~steven spielberg
* the passion of the christ . . . jim caviezel monica bellucci ~ mel gibson

cut to: "a keeper" . . . a wrap!

~ james byron clark ~
august 29th, 2012
los angeles, 90049

/ favorite/ songs
* classic/ films

Bruce Cohn Curtis

Director/Producer

September 19, 2006

Dear Ellie and Byron,

I've come to the conclusion that you two are the Perle Mesta and Truman Capote of Mountain Gate...and beyond! In thinking about the great party givers of our lifetimes, and making the comparisons, I could've said Elsa Maxwell, but was afraid Ellie would throw me off her lovely circular balcony the next time!

Thank you for the lovely "end-of-summer, under-the-stars, like-being-in a villa outside of Rome dinner party". The night was magic.

Love & kisses · B.

P.S. Sorry I had to miss the Cabaret, but the "magic" had left Bijou's lower back...

1015 North Kings Road, Suite 401 Los Angeles, CA 90069.
Tel. (323) 656-4014   Fax (323) 656-4016

~Renaissance Man~

A man, good man, loyalty, handsome, respectful, integrity,
intelligent, helpful, and charming, and a _good_ man.
"A Good Friend"

He is tall/ walks tall/ no nonsense type of guy/
talks the walk/ walks the talk/he said "what
he meant"/ he meant what he said. . .
if he needs you/ he always there/ behind you!
"Standing"

James Westmoreland

"Jim/Gym" early morn/ over-there/ working-out/ discipline.
what you see?/just what you get. . . no "politically correct"
no "p.s. b.s."/ ergo/ i.e no baloney! just **zen**/ no jazz/
"zen-on-the **fist"**/ what you see / *"Jim/Jim."*
"All American"

A Star/ Celebrity/ excellent actor/ known/ aka as well known **"Rad Fulton."**
apropos to: humility compassions . . . obsession perfection/obsession finish
albeit repair-fixer-ups/ problem solvers endeavors / etc. ie. advocacy. . .
'be that way' /'facts on the ground '/. man/woman/God-spiritual mankind
grandeur /artistic/ artesian/ prolific. . . **"Onward Christian Soldiers"**

"Renaissance Man"

you are: *"James Westmoreland"*

James Westmoreland
aka. Rad Fulton   pg. 19

Poem Essay Narrative

james byron clark
~los angeles, 90049~
Sept. 30, 2014

~Summit~

The Way We Were

The way we are . . . where ever you go . . . the way you were . . .
there you go! you can't get-out-of - life without
some tangling horrificus entanglement events accidents albeit
death . . . deaths dangling all there horrific affect/effect you along
striving-fate "travel-in-life" . . . the coping! . . . triumphing!

The measure of man . . . suppositions possibly positive/ negative
your choice and thereby priorities . . . herebys
"talent in your choice" and your "choice in your talent"
your direction/own- director the way of life /Clark Method
"hard-work is a sovereign remedy of a weak-will"
"work-preparation & opportunity so-called luck"
you're so-called / this is. . .
"hi-road" or "low-roads"
"high- roads are few . . ."
"low-roads" are many & crowded . . .
"high -roads" few magnificent - strenuous
challenge below the journey to the mountain . . .
along the climb to "summit"
* "when we meet you at the river"
"God co-driver" is walking with us . . .
what to do ? where to go ! what to choose ?
what way to go ? zen sphinx . . . silence
but . . . "yes" ambeanother chance not "no"
maybe so! alas . . . the mission

james byron clark
august 10th, 2006
~ los angeles ~

* Broadman Hymnal

"THE TRUTH . . . THY WILL BE DONE"

...*Tribute*...
"*Renaissance Man*"

BYRON CLARK   CLAY MITCHELL

Byron Clark/ Monticellonian	mentor	*Hometown/ Monticello* Clay Mitchell

*AD&N/ lone some/ narrative essay poem saga . . .

Scene music: 4:30am smooth longing sound:

As just this/ just as. . . about 4am o'clock fog-chilling/ leeringly sound/
the eerie lonesome/ errey longing/ haunting/ "creosole" smelling ties wistfully/
familiar wandering waiting/ wonderful soft sounds. . . secure sleepy . . .

Scene/ pov: faraway/ glaring small light/ haunting/ hissing/ slow mist-fog-steaming/
dreaming coming on/ and/ an on. . . . .

Wisteria wonderful darkness mysteriously/ black-green train/ clinging clanging crunching /
log-hauling "chuck-chucking" / "ad&n" obdurate-functional choo-choo thru-train/ hamlets
thru-ing crossett/ hamburg/ monticello/ milleu / fountain hill/greenhill / "scrouch-out"/
long prairie / "rough & ready"/ possum valley/ venue/ other miles. . .
just as/ as just this. . .

Scene/ pov: large-bright glaring light/ large front engine/
steaming-mist-fog hissing/ locomotive aka. "iron-horse"/large
"freeze-frame" circa:1864 . . . .

. . .choo-choo train gains "east-west gaines" east toward (to)
west gaines to "ad&n" railway cross-over / north main street/
adjacent "amuseyou film theatre"/ projectionist *percy olsen*/ to
one (1) red-light main street/ to one block "down" / "up" this bluff /
over RR tracks/ to walk onto/ nearby monticello the "square". . .
just two blocks on west gaines right slight downhill to **new "drew theatre"
"texaco gas station," across ***new/ old post office/ with *earl lee harris*/
homer j clark/*guy carter*/ & everybody's favorites. . . as just this/ just as . . .

"Boys of summer" on concrete benches "civic center"/ 4am o'clock
trailways bus/ "dropping" arkansas gazettes/ arkansas democrats/ sat. morn.
the bus-stop. . . after *"mr. bain's"* pool-hall closed 2:00 am. . . as just this
watching/ gamble/ pennies-nickels/ pitch "close to line" on the sidewalk/or
arguing one 1st car/winner arrived 1st "trail-ways" bus got here/from little rock...
boys talking/naughty/ & thinking/about boutique /of our coterie good looking/
voluptuous/ pretty teen-ages girls & women/ from our monticello. . . circa: 1939-45
not un-like other red-stop light/ as monticello arkansas/ ref: "james garner"
"rachel mcadams" "note-book" film... this nostalgia/ "way-off a gone"/ "way of life"
"wherever you go?"/ " there you are!"/ "where did you go?"
just as/ as just this. . .

"Coterie of our best ladies":helen troy martin, betty gibson, margaret ann curry, juanita maxwell,
carmen ramsey, nancy poe wright, mary claire massey, elizabeth ann campbell, betty sanders,
jo beth ellison, sarah tucker, louise funderberg, virginia owens/moon sister/ just a few more of
somewhere/ love / love. . . "where did you go?"

Epilogue/ and best of all:
"boys of summer". . . "honorable mentions" aka dba etc albeit: bobby hardy, billy marks, dansby white, "slick" veasey, billy carson, frank polk, carl lucky, byron howlett, "squirrel" pace, bill bailey, billy rough, johnny bailey, byron clark, reginald trotter, bobby bailey, otis davis, "jelly" sanders, sherwood pace, jimmy bailey, wayne jordan, among all others. . . "wherever you go?" / **God** is hopefully always with **You**. . .

    our names: "Monticellonians"

circa:1920's Crossett. . .

Homer?
two train loads
daily

Addendum: A petit/ paquita/ favor/ flavour / History-trivia *AD&N*

Way back in 1905, the Crossett Lumber Co. of Crossett Arkansas started it's "own little railroad" called (of course) the Crossett Railway. Back then, the railroad mainly worked for it's parent company, transporting logs and lumber around the Crossett Arkansas area. At that time, the railroad was only about ten miles in length.

On May 1, 1912, the line was sold to the newly created Crossett, Monticello & Northern RR. The CM&N planed to extend the line North, up to Monticello, and create a connection with what was then the St. Louis, Iron Mountain & Southern Railroad. Unfortunately, the line only got as far as Fountain Hill before the CM&N ran out of money.

In August of 1912, the railroad was taken over by another owner and given the name Ashley, Drew & Northern. The line to Monticello was finished in 1913 and for the next twenty years, the AD&N continued hauling logs and lumber for the local logging industry. . . P.S William J. Bailey, my Grandfather, Manager-Supt. for "living-in group" incl: families, Operations-working in Crossett Logging Camp, Ark.; in woods with beautiful statuesque, stalwart virgin-pine trees, via lumber/ reseed/ renascent & distribution/ late 1920's-30's. . . Lena was in the "camp" & she was rushed to near the Rose Hospital, Crossett, Arkansas, to deliver her **Son**, baby-boy/ Dec. 6/ born *James Byron Clark*. Now living in Los Angeles 90049. . . i.e., Grandson of William J. Bailey and Bessie Bailey. Lena Bailey Clark & Homer Clark/ at the time resided / Monticello, Arkansas.

*Ashley/ Drew/ & Northern

**Owner, *Mrs. McDougle*, selling tickets/*Frank Polk*/
  sells pop-corn/ picks-up tickets.
***A good man, *Mr.Limebarger*, Construction Company/
  Springfield, Ark./ constr. new Post Office in Monticello, Ark.

james byron clark
los angeles ca. 90049
july 23, 2014

The Ridgeway Hotel
Circa: 1944-45 Monticello, Arkansas

"THE RIDGEWAY HOTEL"

'DEDICATION SPOKEN'

Epilogue:

"...Still staunch and strong
over 70 years long...
as we traverse and travel along the way...
the highways...folkways...and byways
We give a Toast...Kudos...and Accolades
to our 'Crown Jewel...The Hotel Ridgeway' "

youtube: byron clark   james byron clark

august 2, 2011

add-on: a fan of "Tom Cotton"/
warrior/integrity/Statesman...
Senator (R)-Ark.

Jane
~a tribute~

* Jane Oswald

Oct 6th 1935 - 2012

You have been such a part of my life
for such a long time
in so many ways
it's hard to believe . . . you are gone
but no not really
not for long . . .
you belong . . .
"no sad song"
Winchester and Monticello "meeting"
wonderful exciting thrilling
New York City days
and such a "greeting"
we were there to stay . . .
we were enthralled we had it all
and carefree and such a ball . . .

Los Angeles Houston Little Rock Winchester
and back and 'slick' is there . . . *
home earth garden countryside
"autumn leaves twilight- time signs"
ergo: **God's** spiritual heavenly arms
enveloping you . . . it's time to go
"As life's evening sun is sinking low
a few more days and we must go
to meet the deeds that we have done
where there will be no setting sun" *
we love you . . . **God** speed
~ I am ~
Yahweh

Epilogue : a charming wonderful giving bright
funny "will-of-the-wisp" lovely girl a "grand dame". . .
a sensual sexual beautiful woman a Lady . . . Love

~her name is **Jane** ~

*broadman baptist hymnal
* Jane Oswald (Cross)
*'Slick' / Brother / Jane

james byron clark/los angeles/ 90049 3/1/2012

whimsical sonnet : ~ "*America*" ~

Just a toast to "*America*" /land of the freedom
land of the bush/ with a "*bird*" in the bush
but. . . in the "*bush a virgin fair-maiden*"
doth stand. . . a push in the "*bush*" is better with
"*two birds*" in the hands!

Albeit tacit supposition / ref: "*bird*" colloquially i.e.
"*london*"/ completion "*carnal knowledge*"/ecstasy expective
sexually/ excitedly/ sexual a "*wett-warm crouch*"
        Oh My God! omigod/ no push-ups?
                but? / possibly!
Maybe again. . .

I don't know!

a "*bird*"

Saga 2A

Continuing Letters/ Schedules/visiting with
Mike Bailey/ Cuz & Book & Business meeting. . .
Pasadena/Texas

james byron clark
january 9, 2015

pg. 26

PASADENA TEXAS ITINERARY

*Visiting with
Mike Bailey/
Cuz & Book &
Business meeting
"Cyrus The Great"*

SATURDAY JANUARY 28TH

CONTINENTAL AIRLINES - FLIGHT 1007

DEPART - LAX 9:30AM

ARRIVE – IAH BUSH INTL HOUSTON TEXAS   2:43PM

DRIVER PICKS UP AT AIRPORT – "SIGN FOR BYRON CLARK"

TOWN CAR COMPANY – 281-630-1137

LA QUINTA AND SUITES PASADENA

3490 E SAM HOUSTON PARKWAY SOUTH

PASADENA TX 77505

CONTACT - 281-991-7771

MONDAY JANUARY 30TH

11AM - DRIVER PICKS YOU UP LA QUINTA

TOWN CAR COMPANY – 281-630-1137

CONTINENTAL AIRLINES – FLIGHT 1695

DEPART- HOUSTON IAH BUSH INTL 1:15PM

ARRIVE –LAX CONTINENTAL AIRLINES – 3:10PM

EVA CELL 310-403-4785

LALA 562-857-3975

MIKE BAILEY 281-487-2112

Pasadena, Texas. . . etc
Hooters, Texas, Swimsuit Finals

*Jan. 29/2011. . . Lilly St.
Pasadena, Texas.*

byron clark   COPY

July 8th, 2011

Dear Mike,

Good hearing from you! We returned to *Los Angeles* 1st of this week, and really enjoyed our visit to *"Villa D'Este"* (another world) and *Milano*. *"There's no place like home!"* No more European-traveling for me. *"Been there, done that"*…nothing compares to our *Country*, *USA*; even though Los Angeles is becoming *"Third World"*.

Your recent letter being concerned about, *Massoud, National Hero of Afghanistan,* being mentioned in your *Book* and to the *Northern Alliance (United Islamic Front)*. . . believe me, *Mike*, *"not to worry!"* Give me credit, that I would in no way brannish or subvert our project. But, of course, I do welcome any and all *queries*, as we both are on the same page…

As *Struther Martin* said in the movie, *"Cool Hand Luke,"* "its lack-of communication…" and in all due respect to you, and you not knowing or being *aware* of all the *pertinent facts* and *story* of this *"Afghanistan Saga"* is part of the misunderstanding. . . Apropos to *Massoud*, he actually played a leading role in driving the *Soviet Army out of Afghanistan* (see valid informational material to be sent).

I believe you are *confusing elements* surrounding a *Gulbuddin Hekmatyar,* who founded the *Hezb-I Islami Pro-Afghan Communist Party* . . . and the conflict and disputes between*Massoud's* mentor, the revered *"Professor Burhanuddin Rabbani "*(who led the *Jamiat)* and *"Gulbuddin Hekmatyar." Professor Rabbani* was always a leading opponent of the *Afghan Communist Party* and influence.

Hopefully, this will alay *all your fears* as to your *Book* (our project). I am basically on the last page-- the "ending" narrative… Fini!

But we do have about 20 pages in the middle of the *Book* with some editing, scan, and to check-out.

We're almost there….

In Good Health,
Your Cuz,

(James) Byron Clark

addendum: God-blessed savant(ism)
egoism obdurate dogmatic opinionate
message from you. . . Matt. 7:1-3 King
James/ Ref: from jbc

* Ref "Cyrus The Great"

COPY   1

Sunday Feb. 26, 2012

Dear Byron,

I am going to relate to you a thing that occurred about a year ago at a time when I had not heard from you in quite some time.

The thing is that I had a dream, that I am sure was a vision from God.

At the time I was very disturbed by the dream and I called you to see how things were going with* our (the) book on your end.

You can be sure that I am very reluctant to reveal this thing to you because you have lead a very "secular life" and have had very little use for God or the Bible; while I am one of those people your crowd would refer to as a prude.

It is my hope and prayer that working with the book you might develop a personal relationship with Christ Jesus and become a partaker in the life he imparts to all those who believe on him. I would rejoice to see you in heaven at that great reunion where my Daddy and Mama will be along with Aunt Lena. I really don't want you to miss it.

With Love, Your Cuz,
Mike Bailey

"Byron"

~"James Michael Bailey"~
"Christian Warrior"
August 17, 1954 - July 14, 2012

A sensitive, Savant-type of man
marching to his own
'beat of his drum.'
"What's it all about, Michael?"
A statement! A question?
With fledging- tacit unknown
unconscious wonderment . . .
decisions . . . and 'grand missions.'
So, we arrive, sigh, thrive, strive, tithe,
and cry and writhe . . .

~ We Die ~
"Behold, now is the day of Salvation --
Thou shall confess, believing in thine Heart,
that God has raised Him from the dead . . .
Thou shalt be Saved."

The white "Angel" waiting outside to guide you . . .
Michael Bailey, "Onward Christian Soldier"
to be enveloped, inclusive, enclosed above
to the Heavenly Council of the
"Christian Warriors" on High . . .

~ and now ~

"Mighty Christian Warrior" Rises !

~ Cousin ~
James Byron Clark
July 27th, 2012
Los Angeles, Calif. 90049

james byron clark

COPY

<u>Mr. Phillip V.</u>   (Class of 2013)
c/o <u>Dr. Charles Van Riper</u>, Speech Pathology Department
Alumni Relations
1903 W. Michigan Ave,
Kalamazoo, Michigan 49008

"WMU"/ Florida Trip
Kalamazoo
Al Micatrotto
Jack Kürschner
Jim Byron Clark

Dear Phillip V:

Thanks to <u>your</u> belated communique for <u>my</u> appreciation for a
"Dr. Charles Van Riper's" inspiration-discipline for '<u>speech
control</u>' thus; a <u>Life-Changing</u> <u>world</u> <u>for</u> <u>me</u> with "<u>stutter</u>..."
and my venue an <u>actor</u> career... <u>Kudos</u> for '<u>Dr. Charles</u>,' and
so many good thoughts of <u>you</u> and (family)... "Love..." for this
beloved <u>Icon</u>.

"<u>Phillip V.</u>" your appreciation & extensive effort for us...

Sincerely,
In Good Health,

(james) byron clark... 1951-52

P.S. DVD Docu-TV # 4 "Hometown Monticello" "Youtube"
  'First-time thoughts' from WMU a 'student' to
thank you for 'donation' a <u>time</u> to Speech Correction Dept.,
Alumni Relations... "also kudos" to Phillip V...

P.S. #2 Jaime Jeremy, So wonderfully and all is well with you
& family... still I'm "hanging on," Jaime, WMU, & "Dr. Charles..."
  CC: copies... Jaime Jeremy, WMU Alumni, 1903 W. Michigan Ave., Kalamazoo, Michigan, 49008

-HOW IT ALL BEGAN-

Dr. Charles Van Riper

Western Michigan University "Beta Tau" Delta Sig Phi

In Honor & Respect: jbc

Also in 1936, and also in Michigan, a recent graduate of the University of Iowa, Charles Van Riper, Ph.D., was hired to establish a speech clinic and develop a curriculum in speech correction at Western State Teachers College (now Western Michigan University) in Kalamazoo. The success with which this charge was addressed became clear to observers beyond the reaches of Michigan over the ensuing decades as a fledgling profession developed, as audiology emerged as a distinct but interconnected discipline, and as the speech correction program at WMU evolved and became the Department of Speech Pathology and Audiology. *

Byron Clark/ Rosemary Bywaters ... Lois date Jack Kurschner

Students could never *predict* where or how the
next session might be conducted--on a desk top, marching
through the halls, in a coffee shop, at Walwood Hall,
or at Van's house.

All speech correction majors were assigned clinical duties immediately—observing, conducting therapy and doing diagnostics. Clinical assignments included working with stutterers, learning how to count, confront, cancel and modify stuttering behaviors with them.

Student Health and Personnel Bldg., 1939-1950's plus. . .

* WMU Journal of 2012
Speech/Language/Hearing
~Kalamazoo. Michigan~

August/2014
Continuing Saga. . .
Next Page

james byron clark

~Los Angeles 90049~

<u>Rebuttal:</u>   May 16th, 2012

COPY

Michael:

Your insulting statement above is an audacious, ill-informed, and presumptuous_ assumption, apropos: you said, "that <u>I</u> have led a very <u>secular</u> <u>life</u> and have had <u>very</u> <u>little</u> <u>use</u> for <u>God</u> or the <u>Bible</u>; while I am one of those people your crowd would refer to as a prude." Needless to Say, I was surprised, and <u>shocked</u> that you would harbor and/or make such an asinine comment about me. I refute such! "You really <u>don't</u> <u>know</u> <u>me</u>, or any <u>understanding</u> of 'my life and what I am about,' Mike . . ." And especially my <u>relationship</u> with <u>God</u> or the <u>Bible</u>; where I've been, and what I have done! <u>Luke: 6-37</u>.

"<u>Cyrus Endeavour</u>:" Concerning our verbal, tacit, Collaboration agreement, i.e., <u>major time</u> and <u>effort</u> on Editing, re-writes, re-reads, type-pos, and such; And this creative input/output work effort with you was muchly appreciated; along with a goodly /godly amount of time & 'out-of-pocket-expenses,' which I readily assumed . . . But, I misunderstood your (our) interpretation of "our <u>Collaboration</u>." Now this radical change of collaboration-attitude (venue) to your dogmatic, "<u>my way or the highway</u>" behavior leaves me with no departure choice! So Be It.

'Your <u>Cyrus Endeavour</u>' is doable, "and <u>is</u> what it <u>is</u>!" A huge copying task of transferring Biblical sections, references, writing bridges (story lines), and co-leasing Bible Books, chapters and Verses together; and Prophecies. This is most <u>commendable</u> and basically duplications of the Bible.

In my opinion, your book (our book) * would have been much better, improved, more readable and perhaps not as dull, should you been more open-minded, flexible for my thrust, direction and <u>presentation</u> with more *<u>gravitas</u>. Commerciality and salability would be obvious. Thereby, possible 'monies' for <u>your</u> estate and <u>Anne</u> would certainly help . . . Plus <u>your</u> "<u>Legacy</u>."

Love & Compassion,
 Good Luck,

James Byron Clark   http://youtu.be/kp-opkusbee

Cyrus The Great *   pg. 34

byron clark   eleanor vallee

Danilo Zucchetti, General Manager
'Villa D'Este'
Via Regina, 40
22012 Cernobbio
Italy

July 27th, 2012
Los Angeles, Calif. 90049
'Villa Eleanor '
Mountain Gate Estates
2136 Dean Circle

"Villa D'Este"

Dear Mr. Danilo Zucchetti:

This is a most belated communiqué to you. My wife, Eleanor, and I had a most wonderful, charming and knowledgeable visit with you, at 'Villa D'Este.' Thanks to you for your extended effort . . . and 'kudos' for 'Villa D'Este' Staff & all for the appreciated assistance, warmth, friendly, and professional-effort to your valued Guests!

Enclosed, our tasty "DeKuyper Apple Pucker" for our Vodka tonic drinks, as usually within an Apple Martini. As mentioned above, point-of-fact for Enrigco, our favorite Bar-Keeper . . . favorable care of 'Ellie' and I at his fun bar. P.S., this DeKuyper Apple Pucker is a must for your bar, and should be at all 1st Class 'international bars' thru-out Itlay & its Regions .

We had hoped to return to your renowned 'Villa D'Este' this year . . . God willing, hopefully, we will make another memorable visit next year. Thank you for the "Giardini Fioriti Dei Laghi" book. Eleanor is enjoying this book, especially the exquisite flowers of the lakes! ☺

In Good Health,
Sincerely,

Byron Clark ~ Eleanor Vallee

http://youtu.be/KP-0PKvbee   www.rudyvallee.com

pg. 35

BC/EV:ef

" **Whispers in the Attic**"
New Vision Productions

<u>Thoughts, Comments, my Opinion –and Typo Correction</u>   <u>Objectively/ Critique</u> :

(1) <u>Overall</u>, script is structured and tight. Slow beginning – building –beats, good...for pay-off for middle and ending of film. But, <u>shooting scenes</u>, etc., will of course, <u>move the script (film) al</u>ong more so...<u>which is needed.</u>

(2) <u>Needs more Fleshing-Out</u> (all characters)...which I'm certain you will, apropos to earlier scenes of "<u>Joe</u>", subtext, background <u>before</u> the family ("<u>Joan</u>" & "<u>Mary</u>") arrived at <u>Shelby Lane</u> ... flash-backs or present scenes of the "Incident –Accusation" with the "Lolita" 16 year old girl type in the church. You will decide the <u>filmatic</u> – <u>time to reveal</u> <u>such.</u>

(3) <u>About "Mary's" Birth-Wise Clinic</u>? Is the organization "<u>Pro or Anti</u> – abortion"(never spelled out)? Did "<u>Joe</u>" ever counsel there? Why not? What are his beliefs? Different perhaps than Mary's. Is this part of and why the distain for "<u>Joe</u>"? This could be explored more so... perhaps a tacit fear "<u>Joe</u>" will make a move on Joan? Did Mary ever have an abortion? Need more information to round-out "<u>Mary's</u>" character.

(4) "<u>Clayton</u>": About this character...besides having <u>lived</u> in the house, what back-story, experiences, and <u>warped- thoughts</u> and <u>knowledge</u> <u>pushed</u> <u>Clayton</u> into such diabolical delusional killings? Just completely psychotic and sanctimonious, and/or what pushed him completely over the edge? Also, he must have known "<u>Grandma</u>" before...Did Clayton ever have a daughter? Had he ever made a move on "<u>Joan</u>"... earlier days? Jealously? Or some other younger girl? Just on-the-spot killing of "<u>Sean</u>"? Why didn't he let "<u>Sean</u>" go without being killed, and (Clayton) walk away without being seen? Anyway...

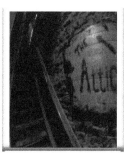

(5) "<u>Tyler & Shelia</u>". Again, need informative, narrative, or film flash-back scenes...fill in somewhere; why is "<u>Shelia</u>" pushing "<u>Tyler</u>" to get counseling help? Her own projection their conflicts? Also, "<u>Tyler</u>" just pops up for counseling from "<u>Joe</u>" ? Where's the meeting(s..the fore-play before the counseling?

(6) <u>Random thoughts – Suggestions:</u>? Seems holes in room could be revealed later after "<u>Joe</u>" feels, and sees "eye's watching" him...<u>closing them</u> and later, holes are open again <u>with eerie film cuts, back and forth</u> – Unknowing & scary! Your choice (of course)... either way is good. Query: Make us more interested in these <u>people</u>? These characters... haven't we "been there-and-done-that-before"? Cardboard-like, pedestrian and almost too familiar to some extent...So, we need <u>character</u> – <u>depth</u> –like scary horrific unknown <u>Hooks, surprises</u>... flash-backs or present scenes to tighten up structure of the script...to give them more substance, <u>gravitas</u>. Suggestion (2): Possible option: With a <u>strong</u> knowledgeable Director and <u>artistic</u> –<u>venturous</u> D.P...go for something "artsy - craftsy", possible vierte film style ... I don't know, maybe documentary in places.
VERTIE

possible ceiling holes open/close

1.

The script, film is very worthy, concept, good and doable. Commercial.

In Good Health,
Good luck and
"Happy Shoot! As Sydney Lumet says!"

Thanks Officer David for the opportunity to read the script, sorry I am a little late with the return.

(James) Byron Clark

JBC:ef

Officer-Security David Ramos/Producer-Writer
Stoney Hill Entrance
Mountain Gate Estates

2.

~Kissable Calves~

Bountiful, Beautiful . . . Tall . . . Proud . . . Aristocratic
18 hands-high -- & confirmation clean along palomino cream
shimmering flowering mane on "kissable- calves"
adaptable feelable smoothing legs . . .

imaginable fanciful heights delights . . .
to behold tight clean fresh smell
smooching stomach tasteful kisses . . .
erotically beautifully oh good creation . . .

a sigh! imagine delights to "behold" . . .
if one is bold / kissable calves
beautiful soft-silky flanks & white thighs
sensual most wet-moist soft thick champagne bush

to cup & to hold & mold . . . if "one is bold"
if "one is so hold . . ." smothered face-down
in "erotic crotch . . ." fanciful fantasy- pure- excite if one is/so bold . . .
circa: greenwich village 1940-1958 etc henry miller . . .
pleasing/pleasurable sexual- decadent milieu venue :
Colloquium (1) also point-of-information pear ass
(2) point-of-fact beautiful apple ass . . .

"Apple cheeks"

pg. 38

james byron clark
~ los angeles, 90049 ~
Oct 9th, 2009

"Kissable Calves & Pear Cheeks"

"ELLIE" REPORTS: BYRON. . .

STARS AND CELEBRITIES – "CELEBRITY SOCIETY" MAGAZINE "THEN & NOW"

<u>Morey Amsterdam</u>: A funny, funny giving man with great sense of humor, was a dear, dear friend of ours. Rudy appeared on "The Morey Amsterdam Show" many times . . . Morey is missed.

<u>Army Archerd</u>: Talented, renowned reporter columnist for Hollywood's "<u>Daily Variety</u>". Army loved **Rudy Vallee** and Rudy adored him . . . and Army featured my husband in many articles – Show Biz!

<u>Robert Goulet</u>: One of my idol's, with the mellifluous, sexy baritone voice, appeared with Rudy on his television show, "<u>On Broadway</u> <u>Tonight</u>" in New York. At the same time Rudy was Starring on Broadway in "<u>How to Succeed in Business without Really Trying</u>" and Goulet was Co-lead in "<u>Camelot</u>" with fabulous, Richard Burton. Yes, those were the choice "Broadway and Show –Time days!" . . . "<u>My Fair Lady</u>" was singing and dancing and holding court up-the-street with Julie Andrews and Rex Harrison (among other shows) . . . 1960's were so amazing and productive!

Phyliss Diller: A top-comedy Hollywood legend. She's a sweetheart and accomplished actress. Also, pianist and artist. To name drop, "Yes, a close friend"! We were honored to have <u>Phyliss</u> share my recent Birthday at The Beverly Hills Hotel on Jan 27, 2011 (Byron says I'm a real Aquarian). Joining us was her friend, Bernie Shine, her handsome Escort . . . a few martinis later!

Jack Lalanne: An Icon and the most famous exercise guru of our generation. Dearest friends, Lala and Jack, who were always at "Silver Tip" (our home) on Pyramid Place, Hollywood Hills. . . . or we were at the Lalanne's beautiful home just below us. The friendship goes way back to San Francisco when Jack Starred in his own Television Show . . .

Ann Jeffreys: A gorgeous, beautiful, talented lady. <u>A Star</u>. A Celebrity. She <u>is</u> Hollywood -- <u>Then</u> and <u>Now</u>. We've had so many good times together, Social, Charities, and Personal. Kudos to our friend, Ann Jeffreys.

Safe, Good, and Happy New Year 2011.

In Good Health,

Love, Love

Ellie

Phyliss Diller

Rudy Vallee *"Icon"*

Ellie Vallee/ James Byron Clark
2011 New Year/Los Angeles, 90049

pg. 39

~ Kenny Tribute ~

"Kenny Kosrog"
June 2006

Life . . . is like a Beijing China Doll –

Even "Kenny" of the Kenny Clan . . .

That wonderful, tough, Marine , sensitive, funny man . . .

Fragile . . . but times

So easy to crack, break –

We have to be watchful, vigilant . . .

Our steps along the way . . .

Whatever cards we're dealt –

"We have to play . . . Each day

Along the way"

"As Time Goes By" ~ Rudy Vallee ~

Knowing and hoping "the pay to play"

Will delay . . .

The Giant-Man " punch-out-the -ticket day" . . . Someday!

~ We love you. You loveable, funny-wonderful, charming,
Sweet . . . ~ "Kenny Kosrog" ~

~ James Byron Clark ~

pg. 40   July 6th, 2006 – Los Angeles, Calif. 90049

"FANTASY SUPPOSITION"

Mary D

Poem is words/ work in progress: ethos

* Buffalo Bill's
   defunct
       who used to
       ride a watersmooth-silver
            stallion ....
  "A gal from Kalamazoo:"
    also far-a-way
     a long-time ago --
      all the time an/
        and place ...**

In Jamaica

Memories/ remembrances/ smiles/ humor/ intelligence
too shorter but & delight-full
   "a gal from 50's ...
    "a girl from Western Michigan College"

God-will be where? I don't know/ where? may be so/ I do know ...
ergo: always a breath "tight-sigh-knot" inside-caring/
Maybe love to be with /you/ every other day ... but

Walking-out art class/ on old campus
A 5-8' estatura extreme real-blonde
Infectious quile smile/ walk-on-off-cover "Goodhouse-Keeping"
A dreaming scene-theme gorgeous
Secret uneffable mistic- milieu ...

A misty dream beautiful sensual erotic sexual/
epiphany-zen breath-taking memories ...
Ideally Love possibly there-is-not-a-day/
that I don't/ think-of-her-that-goes-by/ bye ...
"The Girl from Kalamazoo" ...

Stolen quile/ guild sweet-thoughts/ happenings beguile/
love about could be/ but ... perhaps/ Fantasy Supposition/
addictive perniciously Ideal Love /let-help-let-go & Lost Love ...

Closure. .... Memories ... Cherish

unrequited ...   Her name was Mary ....

* ee cummings /* byron clark   pg.41   ~ james byron clark~ los Angeles calif. 90049
                                                    Aug. 29, 2014

whimsical sonnet :   ~ Sally Jones ~

Here's the bones-of-<u>Sally Jones</u>
born a virgin no runs no hits no errors
died a virgin/ no foul-ups no foul-downs

<u>"Heavenly Home Runs"</u>

(1) Ebbets Stadium Brooklyn New York
     (2) Yankee Stadium New York NY
          (3) "HillBillies" Stadium Monticello Arkansas

Trifecta/triangle/trinity/interrestial-**Sprititually...**
Father/ Son/ & <u>Holy</u> <u>Ghost</u> & **Jesus & God**/ as began creation/
two balls & cane/phallus/possibly tacit mason...
"In The Garden" "<u>Just as I am</u>" "Amazing Grace"
"Old Rugged Cross" plus (1) *   <u>Query</u>
                    &
Yes "<u>**Angel Sally**</u>" no push-ups! or push-downs?

          <u>The End</u>/ Fini

* *Southern Hymnals*

james byron clark
~los ángeles, 90049~
december 2014

"Shane"   Byron

Opening: Championship Pony and Jumpers "Turkey Show"/ Earl Warren Show Ground/ Santa Barbara, Calif./Foxfields Riding Club, Thousand Oaks, Calif. 1982

"SHANE" Winner/ of
CHAMPIONSHIP PONY HUNTER AND JUMPERS
"TURKEY SHOW" 1982

EARL WARREN SHOW GROUND/
SANTA BARBARA, CA. /FOXFIELDS RIDING-CLUB/
THOUSAND OAKS, CALIF...

CHAMPIONSHIP PONYS' HUNTER AND JUMPERS

Ring Attend. ?

"Valentines-Girl" *'13-Hands' high*   *"Shane" Clark Axelrod* *"Turkey Show"* *Santa Barbara, Calif. 1982*

"Shane" *Valentines*

Byron *"Shane"*

pg. 45

"<u>Shane</u>" Forrest Lawn Griffith Show
1981-84's

"<u>Shane</u>" & "Valentine's-Girl"

<u>Byron Clark</u>
Hansen Stables/ 1970-80's

"*Shane*" & "*Valentines-Girl*"/ Forrest Lawn Griffith Ring Show
1981-84's

Sunset Stable "*Friends*"/ *Byron Clark*
Gower/ Hollywood, Calif. 1981

Edgar Root /where?
Baptist Orphanage

"*Byron*" and "*Rufus*"
Hansen Dam Stables / Calif.
1970's

"SHANE"

...Continuing... Drawings/ Art /Poem-Artistics -Pictures/ Saga ... incl. "Samuel James Clark" Axelrod & Shaynin

"Sam" & Mother "Shane"

"Villa Eleanor" Los Angeles, 90049

'Olivia McGuffey' 'Samuel James Clark'

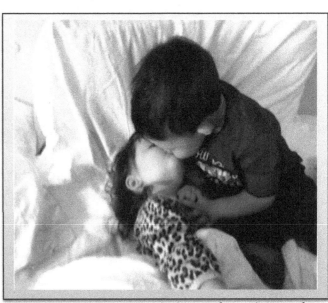

'Olivia'   'Sam'

Saga 4/ Presenting...

"SHANE"

Show Time

Opening: Gallery Drawings/ Art /Poem-Artistics - Pictures/   to see...

Actor John Brandon/"Shane" & Byron
inlc: Irene

"SHANE"
Drawings / Art / Artistics

"SHANE"

"SHANE"

'Shane' Axelrod 11/97

"Shane"

'Shane'

Continuing...

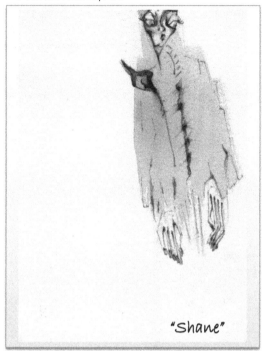

"Shane"

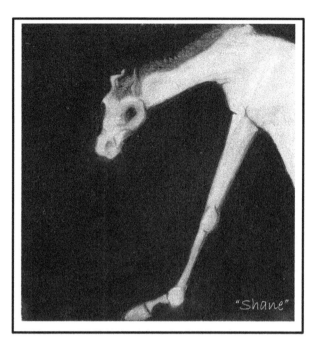

"Shane"

"Shane"

"Shane"

Continuing. . .

"Shane"

"Shane" Axelrod 3/10

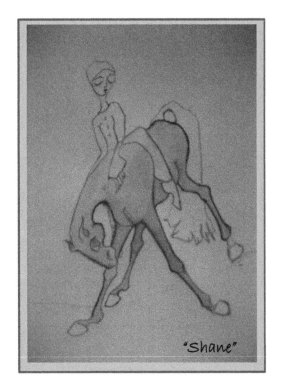

"Shane"

"Shane"

Saga 5/ Now . . .

as per/ Continuing/ Misc./ "Poems of Faces"/Films

And

Mike
Byron

&

"Poems of Faces"/Family/Neighbor

Sarah Tim & Lorraine Lee

pg. 53

Stand By . . .

Miscl . . .

Reginald Trotter "Hometown Monticello"

as per "_emigrate_"/home to _Paris_. . . befriend "Shane"
as her living for 12 years. . .

Good Friends!

*Rancho Mirage
Calif.*

Byron Clark &   Hanspeter Haas &
Eleanor Vallee Clark   Birgitta Haas

Byron Clark

Master-of-Ceremonies Program
"*Operation-Childrens*" 23 annual
luncheon fashion show/ *David*
Hayes fashion/ and *Celebrity* with
Eleanor Vallee /also *Bret Cullen*/
The Regent, Beverly Wilshire. . .
June, 16/2008 at Beverly Hills,
Calif.

Saga/V

pg. 55

"Shane" / Byron

Steve Behar

Byron / "un-name" girlfriend

"GOP"

"Shane" / Theresa

James (Byron) Dean

Dean Chapman   Jim Westmoreland   "Spencer Tracy" Clark/ Byron Clark

SIX-HUNDRED & SIXTY SIX

"666"

"End of Days"

Byron Clark

Joe Turkel

Joe Turkel

pg. 56

"666"
The Man

John O'Connell /
Byron Clark /
Joe Turkel

Tom Doads / Director
Mal Couch
Evangelical-
Communication-
Research-Foundation
Productions. . .1973

IN 1970 IT WAS RYAN O'NEAL AND ALI MacGRAW....
This year is Monie Ellis and Chris Hubbell!

Winter Love

starring MONIE ELLIS · CHRIS HUBBELL · MARLENE TRACY · BYRON CLARK

PG PARENTAL GUIDANCE SUGGESTED
Contains material which may not
be suitable for pre-teenagers

COLOR

PRODUCED AND DIRECTED BY
WILLIAM W. WALL
A FALCON FILMS PRODUCTION

"Winter Love"
aka.
"The Stepdaughter"

Starring:
Chris Hubbell
Monie Ellis

William W. Wall /
Director/ Producer

Hollywood/ Jackson
Hole, Wyoming.
1972~73

Monie Ellis   Marlene Tracy   Byron Clark
(Daughter)   (Mother)   (Father)

pg. 57

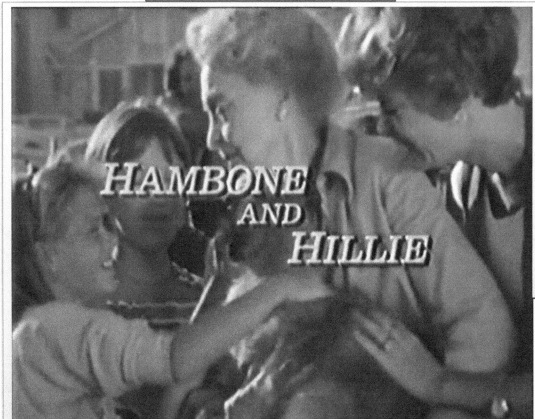

HAMBONE AND HILLIE

Byron Clark Voice/Over for "Trailer" Hambone And Hillie Film

Youtube:
Byron Clark/
Voice/Over
"Hambone and
Hillie"

(S.L.I.P.)

WHAT
DID
MARY
FRANCES
SEE
?

CONTROVERSIAL!
CONTROVERSIAL!
CONTROVERSIAL!
CONTROVERSIAL!
CONTROVERSIAL!

(S.L.I.P.)

EVE BRENT · HY CHASE · MARGARETTA RAMSEY · GEORGE BERKLEY
BYRON CLARK introducing CANDICE ROMAN · DARL SEVERNS
USHER SAVITSKY · RAYMOND STRAIT · HARRY GOLDFARB
JAMES WILSON · LARRY CANSLER & MICHAEL MURPHEY IN EASTMAN COLOR

NOW PLAYING!

Prosecutor.
Buron Clark

George Berkley
Defense

V.I.P.'s

Dinner Parties at "Villa Eleanor"

Mountain-Gate Estates

~Candid~

Martha Selleck (they are Tom's sister & mother), & Phylis Quinn

Eleanor/ Byron/ Lynette Treffinger

Eleanor/ Lora Lee/ Patricia Daily

Family

Jim Westmoreland/
Terry Moore

"Ellie" Vallee/Terry's
Friend

"Peaches"/
Byron

"Ellie"/
"Baby-Bailey"

"Shane"

Bill & Elizabeth

Shaunin Clark Axelrod   Byron Clark

Lala Reyes   Mike Reyes

"Villa Eleanor"/ Dinner Party/ "Poems of Faces"

Dear Ramona & Eleanor

"Ellie"   Steve   Marlene   Sophia

Gail   "Ellie" "Buddy"   Mike

Stella Dr. Howard "Ellie" Loralee Dave

Continuing. . . "Tasteful Flavor & Favor"

Scotty

Dan & Sherry

Stanley&Joyce Black   Bill&Eliz

Leo & Maru

"Ellie" Vallee Clark &   Byron Clark

Byron   Ida Teitelbaum   "Ellie"

"Shane"   Lynette   &

Ramona & Ingmar befriend
"Sam's" born in Paris 5/8/2010

Eva Fairchild
"Villa Eleanor"

Bob & Trudy Bogert

Jack & Lala Lalanne   "Ellie" & Byron Clark
"Thalians-Party"/ Century Plaza Hotel

Nike

June Haver   Byron Clark &
                "Ellie" Vallee Clark

Phullis Diller & "Ellie" Vallee &
              Byron Clark

V.I.P's "Poems of Pictures"... "Villa Eleanor"
Home/Mountain-Gate

Ingmar Brundin

Elizabeth

Steve

Ingmar

~Good Friend~
Excelsior/
Bartender/
"Scotty" Bowers

Sophia

Steve

"Ellie"   "Wild-Bill"

Lynette

Poppy & Fred
Paulos

"Ellie"   and   Byron

~Conviviality~
Joviality/Congeniality
& "Drinks"/more so!
Happy Times/Older Times/
all Good-Looking
People/Persons

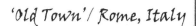

Rome, Italy

'Old Town'/ Rome, Italy

"Ellie" & Byron
Vallee   Clark
Clark

David & Marion
Knutson

"Babs" &

Bernie Fuchs/
Renown
Illustrationist

pg. 65

V.I.P.

Jo-ann

Marilyn Watson

Marilyn Grasshoff

"Ellie"

Party

"Villa Eleanor"

Los Angeles 90049

Grace Scherrer

Ann Jeffreys

"Ellie" Vallee Clark

Byron   "Babs"

David

Marion

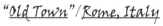

"Old Town" / Rome, Italy

Bernie Fuchs

"Ellie"

Renown Illustrationist Artist

"Bernie"

Eleanor Vallee & Byron Clark

Mr & Mrs Byron Clark

~A <u>Wedding</u>/ <u>Betrothal</u> / "Rev. Donal Keohane"
<u>St Martin of Tours Church</u>/ Sunset Blvd.
Los Angeles, 90049~
(Brentwood Area)

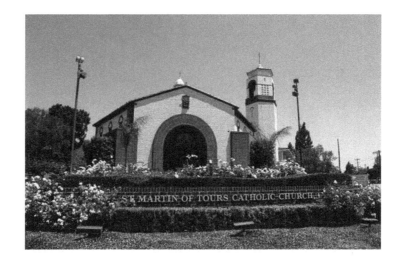

Keep going. . .

BELLEVUE PRESENTS

VALENTINE'S DAY DINNER AND PLAY

LOVE LETTERS

BY A.R. GURNEY FEATURING

ELEANOR VALLEE & BYRON CLARK

THURSDAY, FEBRUARY 14, 2008

COCKTAILS AT 5 P.M. - DINNER AT 6 P.M.- PERFORMANCE AT 7:30 P.M.

And More . . .

Eleanor
Vallee

Byron
Clark

Eleanor
Vallee

Father
Donie

Byron
Clark

Fr.
Donie

Halena

Stella

Father
Donie

Ceasar

Byron

"Ellie"

<u>Where
are they?</u>

Peggy
Lee

Paul
Horner

"Ellie"

Byron

Paul
Horner

Ida

Singapore Airline /L.A enroute to Bangkok / "pretty stewardess"... maybe "Miss Singapore?"

"_East Orient Express_" /
Bangkok to Singapore
Dinner Car/
and Bar Car/ featuring
"well-known _Jack_"/ playing piano!

Byron & "Ellie"

Byron & "Ellie" enjoy "_slinging Singapore_" Raffles Hotel Singapore

"Ellie" Byron &"Lala" Mandarin Oriental Hotel Bangkok.

Arrive to Singapore / East Orient Express/ farewell famous butlers and attendants...

"Lord Byron"

pg. 70

Hotel Lord Byron

"Eleanor Vallee" Clark

Byron Clark

"*Honeymoon*"

Rome, Italy

Nicole Greicco

"Eleanor Vallee"

Lounge Bar

~Fun & Conviviality & "*Nicole*" & Others~

"Honeymoon"/<u>Planning</u>/<u>Travelling</u> to Rome, Italy

Eva Fairchild/
P/A
Realtor/Mogul

Byron

"Ellie"

"Three Musketeers"

"<u>Honeymoon</u>"
Rome, Italy

Byron & "Ellie"
"Spanish Steps"

<u>Cardinal Sodano</u> Blessed
"<u>Eleanor</u> & <u>Byron</u>"

<u>Vatican</u>

"<u>Honeymoon</u>"

Fan?

"Ellie" & Byron
Vatican
Palazzo

pg. 72

Nicole Griecco
"Hotel Lord Byron"
Roma, Italy

Byron
Clark
Los Angeles

Nostalgia Addendum

~Actually another additional <u>Nostalgia Addendum</u>/ Oxymoron
    Patterns of 'Styles' of Nostalgic suppositions repeat
"Poems-of-Itself" styles of stirring-emotional of 'love of acumen
    valuation/ <u>Rhymes of History</u>-- 'Simplicissims' visual of culture . . .
                    "<u>Poems of Life</u>"
                    "<u>Pictures of Poems</u>"
                    "<u>Poems of Words</u>" ~

Nostalgic 5 degrees: " ? " <u>Alice Lile</u> / beautiful lady/Hope, Ark . . . Query?

"What is this really mean"?

"I don't know"!

whatever you go/ there you are

Dr. Howard Murad

Shaynin (Shane)
    Clark Axelrod

jbc
los angeles
nov. 2014

ARNETTE JENS

"POEMS
OF
FACES"

1960's

Ben Tucker

*Arnette Jens/
Actress/Painting
Drawing/Dancer*

Query?

*Ben Tucker/
Actor/Writer Novels*

*Lee Ballard
Singer/
Actress*

*George
Harwell
Actor/
Singer*

LES BALLARD

GEORGE HARWELL

pg. 74

Michael Keep (Capanna)
Actor

Perry Lopez
Actor

Dean (Bill) Chapman
Actor/Singer/Realtor

jud taylor as "goff" the american

Jud Taylor
Actor/Director

pg. 75

Shaynin Clark
Axelrod

Deborah
Morgan Axelrod

Byron Clark   Good-buddy   Jim Harris

Byron Clark   Teresa Victor
P.A/Celebrity   Nathaniel
Lande

Byron Clark   Alex Olivia

Wedding/Montauk

Carole Hemingway
Writer

ABC/Radio Talk Show

'Alex Olivia/ Dino'Alexander
1950's-60's/Actor

'<u>Stephanie Edwards</u>'/Actress/
<u>Celebrity</u>/Spokeswoman "<u>Rose Parade</u>"
1960's-70's-80's 90's & <u>etc.</u>

Sally Stark/
Actress/Comml./ 'Soaps'
1960's-70's

Eli (Steve) Behar/Actor/Owner
'Tax Shelter Rest.' Idyllwild, Calif.

Virginia Carey   &   "Cal" Carey

"Ellie"   Byron

"Ellie"   &   "Scotty"

CLUB & SPORTS **SOCIETY**

"Ellie" Vallee Clark & Byron Clark
Enjoying/ "Hotel Negresco"/ bar
Nice, France

Trudy Bogert "Ellie"   Ruta Lee   Margie
          Vallee Clark   Peterson

pg. 78

'Lisoniel'/ Vero Beach /formerly Pittsburg, Pa./
beautiful strong "dogs"/ names...

Erin   Kelley   Justin   Jessica   Colby   Aaron

"Samarai"

"Maximus"   "Bear"   "Lucy"   "Winston"

Linda & Herb Conner

"Linda, dear friend/many special-times all we shared"/745 No Alfred/
Los Angeles 1970's

"Spencer"
Tracy   **Byron Clark**

Bill Bailey

Special remembrance my 1st cousin/<u>**Bill Bailey**</u>
~"Wild Bill"/this quiet strong good way~

Byron &
"Ellie" Vallee Clark
& Princess

"will trade to 'your'
Rolls-Royce!"

(Not really!)

Good Buddy &
Sherman Oil Co.
Texas
~Mogul~

Janice & Neal Lynch
Branson, Missouri

Allegory

Saga: also faraway a long-time-ago--
all-the-time/ and time-is-life an/
and place/ past/ present/ now... **now**

"**Life is Probation**" slowing down/
moving on/ "prophecy-advocacy" ideas/
"probies" not _professionals_/ but **amateurs**...

* "He was **handsome man**
                    and what i want to know is
and how do you like your **blueeyed boy**
Mister Death!" *

/ ee cummings

jbc/ 2014
los angeles

Query?
Bruno/NJ/
NY?

"_John Byron
Clark_"
ORD
Kerns UT.
?

"Good Buddies"/Guam
1945-46

Mike Rettig/ South Dakota

Jim (Byron) Clark
Monticello Ark.

Attach: 147th Air Communications 20th Air Force Squadron/Guam

81

"POP"

~ Homer J. Clark ~

Homer (James) Clark

"That is, what I call him '*Pop*'
not a day goes by
that I don't think of him . . ."
"*Homer J. Clark*" . . . my "*Pop*"

My "Pop," I was so proud of him . . .
far-away mystery yet unknown . . .
Yakima,Washington , but not known . . .
Hanford area, my "Pop" was a train engineer
this confidential huge defense-work compound
toward -end of World II . . .

~ Depression-time dependable
economical-sacrifice signature copious. . .
All in two years, only two visits
returned back to Monticello
that "Pop" decided to come home
and be with Lena & Byron . . .
"So on this journey trip home through
U.S.A.--Kansas on the train on the plain
between Colby & Olathe/ pain . . . yes, suffering" ~

(James) Byron Clark

Horrific, horrificus, horrible . . .
On February 26ᵗʰ, 1945 . . .
"My Father, Homer J. Clark,
was to arrive to home, Monticello . . .
But, it happened a "different way . . ."
and then . . . "completed . . ."
his journey finishing to home."
* "would you know my name if saw you in Heaven"

"Byron"

PS epilogue: painfully to a dark-side "unfortunate"
a fight . . . then just very only later "evil-demonic" ugly knife attack
wbruce(n). . . grasping gasping. . . then acquiesce light "passing-over"
to Heaven . . ."angrily , not wanted Homer J. Clark to go . . " I'm pissed off!
but, "God's Thy Will"/. . . or? "Onward Christians Soldiers"

* "*Mary Stallings*"
"*Eric Clapton*"

fini

~James Byron Clark ~
February 17ᵗʰ, 2010

*Saaa/ "Life is Probation" slowing down/
moving on/ "prophecy-advocacy-ideas"*

"Family"
Last Christmas 1944
Monticello, Arkansas
508 Boyd Street

Son   "Pop"   Mother

"Samuel James Clark" Axelrod (Helguerra)
" Papy" James Byron Clark

Homer James Clark

James Byron Clark   Lena Bailey Clark

olivia & sam 2013
another year of love

Sam/ born Paris/ 4yrs Los Angeles

~POEMS OF LIFE~

"The End"   LEGACY

. . . *Fini*

"Th-at's Th-at's That's All Folks!"

The End

"Baby-Bailey"
Princess

"Peaches"
Black-Eye Peas

"SWEET"

"ELLIE"   "Byron"

Today and always...

"*Poems of Faces*" / *Words* / "*Poems of Life*"

L to R: Webb Lowe,   Carol Channing,   Margie Petterson,   Eleanor Vallee,
      "Ruta Lee" Lowe,   Wally Seaweld,   Bob Petterson,   Byron Clark

Brunch by "Ruta Lee" for VIP/ "Thalians" party/ at
Century Plaza, Century City, CA./next day

To Eleanor and Byron
With Best Wishes,

Statesman / Integrity / outward Excelsior ...
"could have been" / "would have been" "should have been"...
wherever you go / there you are.... but? .... but, Now! Supposition:
Hubris/Chameleon!

pg.87

jbc/ev
revision: Jan 8/2019
los angeles 90049

Appendix... 2

"Hometown Monticello" Arkansas

Top/ L to R: Helen Troy Martin, Elizabeth Ann Campbell, Billy Carson, Byron Clark, Jo Beth Ellison
Bottom/L to R: Alice McClerkin, Carmen Ramsey, Betty Gibson, Louise Funderburg, Juantia Maxwell

"Monticello High School" Country-Club Supper/ partially Reunion

"Nostalgia-Time Twilight"

From a happy wonderful fruitful studious * thoughtful few years a-go/
A far-a-away/ but now/ after away/ then now/ but now/ twi-light
& thoughts / "Hometown Monticello" /& Spiritually Deity . . . @
Time-Line/ Rod Serling-ism "Twilight-Zone" . . .
God Love to You & Cherish . . . . .Byron

* maybe/ not me!

pg. 88

*james byron clark
los angeles, ca
jan. 9, 2015*

~Tribute~

*Judge Roy L. Sanderlin/Drew County/Monticello, Arkansas. "God-fearing..." Good-Man/ integrity/ hard-working man & well-liked by all constituency... Roy L. Sanderlin elected Judge & served over 14 years approx. 7-8 terms unopposed! His Administration successfully in-frastructure/ structure/etc highways-roads/social services & venues. **Honorable Judge Roy L. Sanderlin**, also well known in Arkansas, Little Rock, & in South East Arkansas... His "word" is what he says/ what he says / "words" is what he means!...with action...

'Respectfully'...and I was proud of my Step-Father... his name is (was)... "Judge Roy L. Sanderlin"/plus...

Byron Clark

Sibling: Roy L. Sanderlin, Jr./Reba Sanderlin Harper/ Colleen Sanderlin ___?/ among, families and etc...

*District Court of Drew County

james byron clark
los angeles, ca
feb. 9, 2015

Other Books by Byron Clark/Poems
trifecta/ Book's/triad

(1) <u>A Surrender to the Moon</u>/ "Our Life"
(2) <u>Best of Poems of 2005</u>/ "Vigil Ode to Ben Tucker"
(3) <u>International Who's Who</u>/ "Awakening Love"
(4) "Shane"/ now quartet
　　International Library Poetry/Howard Ely/ Editor
　　One Poetry Plaza/ Owings Mills. MD 21117

"<u>Cyrus The Great</u>" Ahasuerus/ a Persian Warrior/famous
　　about 549/Biblical Book/Prophecies/References/
　　by Mike Bailey/ Byron Clark/ Collaborator-Writer
　　Avid Readers Publishing Group

Only "last page" and is "next page"

"Zweck" & "La Ultimo"

"Fini" & "The Last"

Allegory Nostalgic Item Narrative fact-of-info-Poem/ essay: '4-5 degrees-of-life.' Huckabee/Clinton "Boys State"/ Little Rock, Arkansas/both (2) 'Hope,' Arkansas...But, b.c. b.f. i.e. Byron Clark* / not now 'now then' before (them) few years ago "Boys State" / Little Rock. . . Hoping & not 'Hope'/ Actor/ Monticello, Arkansas/ "Hometown Monticello"'...

Politicians/Actors ergo: charming & combining supposition conniving 1st cousins many self-believing the b.s hubris spinning "Gravatis"... all members of the 'goofy' Clans! Congress? Rogue Leadership varied wastefull tax payers/deficit...remedy Congress/too many "Lawyers" ..."Time-Limit Terms"!

*Sponsor: "American Legion"

Genießen. . . Godere. . . Jouir. . .Enjoy!

Eleanor Vallee Clark

Byron Clark

&

"Peaches"

"Ellie" Vallee

&

"Baby-Bailey"

"Poems of Life"
"Faces of Poems"
"Poems of Words"

Coping:
"You spend your life/ spend of strive & thrive/ and find your length you find (out) your 'weakness' has become/ the 'pillar' of your strength......" "your stutter!"

"Father" "Son" & "Holy Ghost"
Shin/Shaddai/Hebrew aka "God"

jbc/ anonymous/Bible maybe

~ Memorial~ Tribute~
Family

My dear Uncle Velmer & 'Kitty' Clark/ my uncle/ Homer's older brother //Sons 'Jimmy' & Peggy(wife) Clark /Carrol Clark & Cousin Sue Clark /Daughter . . .

"Honorable/lovingly/ this quiet strong good-way/ and God-loving spiritual-way of life". . . Proud of you!

Hamburg, Arkansas

-Remembrance-

Sad/ Ethos/ Tragic... P.o.v. / The treacherous fate-car accident/ teen-agers driving from Monticello to Warren /So. East Arkansas/on a sunny day 1941 when "loose-gravel road" "grabbed -up" 1938 Pontiac/& flipped- up/& rolled-over couple of times// fatally!

Surreal.....   Freeze-Frame

Claude Hudgens, Jr   Billy Secret/aka Secriet ?
Angel /Young Teen-agers   Angel/Young Teen-agers
Cherish/Posthumous   Cherish/Posthumous
       1941   1941
Monticello, Arkansas   Hamburg, Arkansas

"Never Gone... Always Here"

jbc
rev. oct,18, 2018
los angeles, 90049

"*Faces of Fun*"
"*Words of Poems*"
"*Poetry is Fun*"

"*Molson*"/ *featuring* "*smiles*"/ model: *Byron* / Photo: *Carter Jones*
(comml & print)   circa: New York, New York 1958-60's
~Manhattan~

A far-away fun years ago/ now there now here/ Nostalgia pertinent
perfect fun-times ago/ whimsical & humorous! Folds & Flow & Freedom/
Flavor & Favor & Fave-Fun... "Poems of Life"/ "Faces of Poems"/
"Poems of Words" & "Poems of Fun"... as per/ "The Last Picture Show"
not unlike/ "Closure" erao: saaa @ journey via Monticello Ark. WMC
Kalamazoo/ New York City & Los Angeles Calif. 90049 /Brentwood area
continuing until... whenever...

Enjoy Book

jbc
3/4/2015
los angeles. 90049

"Baby-Bailey"/Maltese (Royal)/"Ellie's" 'Baby-Bailey' our-
child-deity is adorable, loving, & sometimes, ornery!.. Alive!...

pg.95

P.O.V./Sonnet: "Older man" Mr. Clark/ "Baby-Bailey"
doggy/aqua green pool...On-top "Mountain-Gate"/ gazing
north-horizon-majestic santa monica montains/
Ghostly 40-plus hump-back gray- whales/"circus parade" milieu
magic "guardians"!... Angel-'Watchers' /Serenity/ "As Life's
evening-sun is sinking-low" ..."Just As I am" *
              ~JES–US~

*Baptist Hymns   jbc/rev.07/18/2018

EPILOGUE: REMEMBERING... "AND SHE CAME INTO MY LIFE...
BEAUTIFUL, TALL, ARISTOCRATIC HEAD SO PROUD"...
MY WIFE
"LOVE, LOVE... TODAY AND ALWAYS"

~ELEANOR VALLEE~

'My Angel'/Cherish/Posthumous/ December 7, 2015

CPSIA information can be obtained
at www.ICGtesting.com
Printed in the USA
LVHW061125160119
604046LV00001B/1/P

9 781612 862606